God, I'll Take Those Crumbs
A Mother's Resolve

By L.S. Reed

Nashville TN

First Printing: 2015

ISBN 978-1-943616-01-5

MAWMedia Group, LLC
2525 Somerset Drive
Nashville, TN 37217

www.mawmedia.com

Cover photo collage by Melanie J. Pullman

DEDICATION

This book is dedicated to the memory of two of my four sons, the late James Howard Williams JR. and the late William Austin Williams.

ACKNOWLEDGEMENTS

I would like to thank God for the courage and strength to write this book. I also thank my two remaining sons, Juan and Michael for their unwavering support. Thanks Michael for much of the typing and Juan for the lovely flowers to cheer me. Thanks Vaughn and Carl for helping me to remember. Thanks Roy for the pictures. I thank my spiritual family Trish Nealey and the Park Hill Prayer Warriors. I thank all of my family and a host of friends, clinicians and others whose support I felt but are too numerous to mention by name. A special thanks to Ms. Dorothy L. Burse for encouragement throughout my journey and a true go-to person when I need inspiration in difficult times. Ms. Burse has a knack for saying the funniest things that make you laugh and think all at the same time. It's called whit. Thanks for your kindness to my late son James Williams during his long illness. Sincere thanks to Ms. Bettye Marcanno. Bettye offered continued support and medical advice during the remaining days that my son was cared for in my home. Also, I am grateful to the doctors, medical team, and staff of University Hospital.

Table of Contents

Foreword

The author speaks to us initially, one would consider as an imaginary abstract, an oxymoron (if you will) as if were of being poor, but extremely happy. Throughout the above, she does give us the delicate and loving example of the, crumbs, that fell from her Master's table.

Realistically, this book has the nuances of a daunting, Shakespearean novel, the gentle and consistent love of a father, the integrity and affluent and lady-like manners of her mother instilled throughout her (crumbs from the Master's table) The foundation from both parents, gave her the strength to withstand the very ferocious thinking and abusive husband, and other men, that crossed her path, with the same sad and perfidious characteristics.

The events were sometimes compelling and riveting, but because of the precious and loving crumbs that fell from the Master's table, the author soothes our conscious, with an extraordinarily and poetically artistic description to soften the blow of the tragic events in her life i.e. abusive men, two talented sons, with mental and drug abusive struggles, that ended in death for both. All of which was overwhelmingly devastating to her as a mother.

This book, will keep your undivided attention, without a doubt, from start to finish. Enjoy!!

Bettye Marcanno RN, BSN, CCNP

Introduction

It was late in the evening in the summer of 2009. I was having a difficult time falling asleep as is usually the case. I suffer from a malady called "Sleep Apnea". As I lay there in my bed I began to compare my sleep disorder to what writers sometimes experience while trying to write books. Sleep is anything but normal for writers. They have these unusual sleep patterns and often a flight of ideas along with it. Then there are those Kodak moments when a flash a genius happens and voila; a title for a new book or poem. If I could give the irregular sleep patterns of writers a name I would call it "Writers Apnea". Oddly enough I fall into both of these sleep patterns. I have come to realize that I am a minute woman as well. I have to be on call with my mind twenty four seven. I never can predict when I will think of something useful for one of the several books I am writing. I am in my sixties and my memory is not as keen. So when an idea happens I need to be able to record it on paper very soon so I don't forget it. I try very hard to keep some paper and a pen with me the majority of the time. My son William was a writer too. He would write on whatever was handy at the time. I retrieved some of his poems included in the bonus section of this book from the surface of brown paper bags, scraps of old newspaper and greeting card boarders. William simply used what he had available to him at the time.

The title for this book was a God idea and is based on the familiar text of scripture found in Matthew 15:27 that say, *"Yes, Lord, but even the dogs eat the crumbs from their master's table"*. Both my parents are deceased. My parents were nominal Christians. They never preached to me, but I just knew that they believed in God. They stayed at home on Sundays for years, but my Father insisted that my brothers and I while very young should go to church. I was about eight or nine years old when I began attending the neighborhood church about two blocks from our house on Martindale. It was a Methodist church. I liked it well enough and the people were nice to me. My parents probably heard the scripture about the woman begging for crumbs from the master's table. And if they had been religious folk they would have also appreciated my use of crumbs in this book. They would have liked my inference to making cornbread with the crumbs as well. My parents may possibly have desired to make a whole loaf of cornbread with their crumbs from the master's table. But in my opinion they may have only ended up with half a loaf. From that half of a loaf my brothers and I were then expected to make our own cornbread. As for what happened with the missing half from my parent's cornbread? It represents the unfulfilled hopes and dreams for my brothers and me. Maybe some of my parent's unfulfilled dreams too. From what I learned about God as a young girl gave me the desire to make my own cornbread. Even as a little girl I felt the there was something different about me. Different as in I never felt that I was quite as good as other girls I knew. I now know that "different" meant I was not a daughter of privilege. I was by the standards of my genre' just an average normal "negro", who, was growing up in my parent's home. There were no trappings of the finer things of life in my humble surroundings. I wore hand-me down dresses. Some of them came from the second-hand store and a few were like new. My momma had acquaintances and even some family on daddy's side from the middle class (women of privilege) and some she met at the grade school I attended. They would give my momma some of the dresses their daughters had out grown for me to wear. The dresses were clean and even beautiful, but they were hand-me downs. As I got older it didn't take me very long to realize that my daddy was what most folk considered to be, among the "working class poor". For some that may have been debilitating but none of these things could stop me from making my own cornbread.

My parents always said that I was a survivor. The reason of course was that I was born at the tail-end of the "Great Depression" era. They had big hopes for me. So I tried extra hard to please them. My daddy called me his "Princess". I thought that was silly because I never really felt like a princess. In fact I hated who I was. I hated my dark complexion and thick hair. And even more I hated those hand-me-down clothes.

I developed a love for reading and writing when I was in elementary school. Some of my favorite authors were Langston Hughes; Paul Lawrence Dunbar; Robert Frost, and Phyllis Wheatley etc... The Bible became one of my favorite books growing up. I was smitten and "head over hills" in love with Jesus from reading the Bible stories.

I truly loved music when I was growing up. My exposure to music, literature and religion as a child growing up serves as a backdrop for much of my creativity and inspiration as a writer. Among some of my favorite singers were singers like Perry Como; the Lawrence Whelk Show singers; Johnnie Mathis; Barbara Streisand; Nancy Wilson and many other greats from that time span. I was crazy about the popular dance shows American Bandstand and Soul Train. Daddy worked as a janitor for the RCA record company when I was growing up, so he brought me lots of free records home every week. I had lots of "new releases" in my collection. I may not have had much of the things the daughters of privilege had growing up, but I did have bragging rights with my music collection.

In the "Bonus Section" at the end of this book I have included a short paper written by my son James and some poems my son William wrote. I took the liberty of replacing some of the crude language in Williams' poems because of the Wide range of possible readers of this book. Several of my poems are included and a chapter my son Michael requested to contribute toward completion of this book. My dream is to use the majority of the proceeds from the sale of this book to set up a scholarship fund for at risk youth in memory of my two sons James and William. If you have purchased this book I thank you for moving the reality of my dream one crumb closer! I invite you the reader to feast from the Master's table and if inclined to do so, gather some crumbs along the way. From the Master's crumbs, may you gather courage and hope, and at the end of the day may the giver and sustainer of life Jehovah Jirah, turn your crumbs into cornbread. May you be filled over and over again with more than enough!!

Chapter 1: My Parent's Half Loaf

Unlike most of my summers growing up in Indianapolis, It was an unusually hot sultry summer day; the year was 1954. My parents said I was born there in Indianapolis. That must be so because I never knew a life outside my hometown as a little girl except when our family went to visit relatives in Ohio. I must have been nine years old at the time. I remember that age because It was at the age of nine that I was molested and almost raped by a stranger in the park across from where we lived at the time.

On today as was usual, I was engaging in a favorite past-time of mine, which was, listening to music and sitting in my rocking chair just rocking. My brothers, Vaughn, Roy, and Glen, were doing their own thing. My brother Carl was passing time in his make-shift lab reading Popular Science books and making stink bombs or some other weird experiment. My daddy was at work. He worked seven days a week as a janitor. It was an honest living and got the bills paid and to boot he got free records as a bonus. My momma was busy as usual on the party-line. Gossiping was her thing. But she kept busy with her craft work and playing cards most days.

I settled down into my rickety old run down rocking chair. It happened to be my chair of choice and it was always right there in my reserved spot in front of our second hand TV/Stereo console. My days passed by unencumbered and predictably serene there. As I settled back and listened to music my mind took flight and drifted into an almost magical world of make believe. Music was my escape back then. Those melodious renderings and lyrical musings were to me what reading is to most folk. As I sat listening to music I became a time traveler to faraway places beyond the dreary reality of the moment. And I was a princess with opulence, surrounded by my court. I travelled to exotic places filled with charm and adventure. And I lost myself in the breath taking panoramic landscapes of beauty and brilliance. My travels took me far away from the dreary familiar trappings of our old house. There was not much happening here in the lackluster of these walls. They were just ordinary rooms decorated with traditional wallpaper and windows trimmed with lead paint. The living-room was no different with its carefully arranged area rugs and swept clean linoleum covered floor. Today our style of furnishings would be called eclectic, but back then it was just mixed up old furniture that was functional but didn't match much. The furniture like most everything else in our house was second hand too.

As I continued listening to music and rocked, I drifted away on one of my adventurous journeys. And I began to once again experience the vicissitudes of a better life outside of my own reality. Once again I was a real princess with all of the trappings of the rich and famous...

That old golden blond rocker squeaked under my weight in time to the rhythms of the music. The louder and faster the beat, the harder and faster I rocked. The force of the rocking movements scooted the rocking chair from in front of the console to a distant spot across the room. There was a pattern to my rocking that was similar to the precision of an assembly line worker and the determination of an autistic child. I was never diagnosed with Autism, but maybe I could have been. So I continued rocking across the room, stopped, lifted the rocker up, and place it back in front of the console again and again. I did this for hours on end finding much pleasure in it all. For as long as I can remember nothing else gave me so much pleasure. I was truly grateful that my daddy worked as a janitor for the RCA Record Company. And glad that for as long as I wanted to, I could pass the time away in that old rocker listening to music.

My second favorite past-time growing up was dancing. I was pretty good at it. If I wasn't rocking, then for sure I was dancing. I only did something different if my momma or daddy wanted me to do something or I had homework to do. I learned most of my dance steps from friends and our next door neighbors the Burse family. There were three girls in their family. That made it great for me! I had two sisters from an earlier marriage on Momma's side that were way older than me, but no sisters to grow up with in my present family, just four brothers. The Burse girls and I were always at each other's house dancing or doing girly things. Ms. Burse could cut –a-rug too. My momma wasn't much of a dancer. At least I never saw her dancing.

Crafts or card games was her favorite past-time thing to do. I was really great with the "Cha-Cha" dance steps. Some of the other dances I liked was the" twist"; "Madison"; "Slop"; "Mash Potatoes", and the "Chicken". My parents approved of dancing so I danced as often as I liked. I even thought of becoming a "Ballerina" once. I abandoned that idea when I realized my pigeon toed feet and long torso figure weren't at all suitable for it.

There was a house in my neighborhood just two houses down from ours that had a favorite dance spot. The family that lived there operated a "Ma-Pa" store on their property right in back of their house. It was fully loaded with all sorts of fun stuff including a fantastic Juke- Box. Lots of us neighborhood kids gathered there most days after school and week-ends to spin records for a nickel. Summers were the best! I could stay longer at the Spot in the summer cause the daylight lasted longer and all. And living so close to the dance spot made it easy for me to go there most school days during lunch time as well.

On school days, my brothers and I had to come home for lunch. My daddy couldn't afford lunch money for the five of us. But daddy always made sure we had lunch food at home and a hot meal at dinner time.

One of the fondest memories about daddy was that when I was very young he would bring a glass of orange juice to me every morning before he left for work. It didn't matter that it was so early; my Father left for work around four in the morning. I missed the morning juice when I got older. There was always plenty of snack food to eat in our house. I suppose that is where I got the habit of munching throughout the day. I can truly say that our bread and water was sure.

My daddy was never in the military so we weren't Army brats. But my daddy ran our household like an army drill sergeant. He did all of the grocery shopping too. He even made the shopping list every week. We could just about predict what he would buy from week to week. My daddy was a sort of philosophical man as well. He would find famous quotations and write them on paper and post a different quote each week to the kitchen doorway to make sure we saw it whenever we went into the kitchen. I grew fond of those quotes and over time developed my own brand of philosophy. That was not the only thing daddy posted either. On Saturday he always posted a menu for Sunday dinner. That was predictable too. My daddy was good with finances and budgeted religiously. As me and my brothers grew older daddy gave each of us an allowance of fifty cents every Friday. Of course we were expected to spend it wisely and we each had assigned chores to earn it. Daddy gave my momma five dollars a week for her allowance. She didn't have to earn her allowance though. The catch was that she was supposed to budget the five dollars so it would last for the whole week. If momma ran out of money before the week and asked daddy for more she had to have a real good explanation for it, and she had to pay daddy the extra money back. My daddy actually had a "little black book" with an "IOU" list in it! I realize now that daddy was just being frugal. But the meticulous regiment of my daddy's money matters had sort of a negative effect on me growing up. So to this day I hate budgeting and I rarely attempt to balance my check book.

I suppose daddy had good reasons for how he dealt with my momma in money matters. My momma was terrible at managing money. To make things worse she had a gambling habit. She didn't have a lot of money to gamble with; just small bills. She played "Nickel Tonk" a lot and belonged to a card party club for as long as I can remember. When the time came that me and my brothers were all in school, momma took a job as a School guard to finance her habit, and other things her weekly allowance didn't cover. She taught me and my brothers how to play cards, but we weren't allowed to gamble. We played for fun. Momma would buy all sorts of board games for us to play with. I believe momma loved having kids around because she became a volunteer with the local scout troop and became a real Den mother. Our house became a popular hangout spot for the kids in our neighborhood. If we weren't dancing, we enjoyed playing board games or cards. On the other hand,

I was always hungry for momma's affection growing up. My being the only girl made it easy for daddy to make on over me. But momma seemed real busy with her volunteer work and my four brothers most days. My brothers seemed to be having all the fun. My brothers got to go outside and do fun things like climbing and hiking and making Go Carts to race from old wood and things. Momma restricted me from those things. She said it was because I was a girl. I recall as a toddler momma even forbid me to crawl on my knees. She spanked me if she caught me crawling. She said I would make ugly scars on my knees if I crawled on them.

She was determined to make a little lady out of me in spite of my preference to be a Tom Boy instead. Momma tried everything she knew how to get me to like girly things. She even took me to a woman who did needle work and crocheting for her to teach me. I pretended I couldn't catch on so she stopped taking me there. All I really wanted to do was to have fun like my brothers did. Then one day out of the blue momma announced that I was enrolled in the Blue Birds; a club just for girls. I was ecstatic! At last I had something to do that was more to my liking. And my brothers couldn't do it; this was just for me! I recall momma taking me to the meetings and dropping me off there. I was really shy back then and didn't like the way the other girls made fun of me sometimes. So Momma decided that she would start staying with me when I went to the meetings. I didn't mind their indoors activities, but the outdoors was a different story. I thought I was going to get to do things like my brothers did during our outdoors activities. But somehow they made it into girly activities instead. I was sitting in the grass at a Day Camp once and got the worst chigger bites ever. After that I was cautious about sitting in grass.

The next summer my momma went with me to an overnight camp for a whole week. It was some place in Indiana. There was actually a cemetery on the camp grounds; it was supposed to be the burial ground for some of the relatives of Abraham Lincoln. That did not go too well with me. I was really spooked after finding that out. I recall wetting the bed just about every night I was at that camp. It was usually pitch black at night when I had the urge to use the outdoor facility. So I was too afraid to go there and ended up with a wet bed instead...

After trying for two years to get me to metamorphose into a little lady momma finally gave up. Yea!! At last I could join in with the games of marbles, ride go-carts, walking on home-made stilts and stomp cans onto my shoes. I could do backyard camp outs... Well not exactly the backyard, but momma and daddy agreed that I could camp out on our front porch with my younger brother Glen in the summer when it got extremely hot at night. The best thing was that I never was coerced to become a part of any Girls clubs again and momma let me do most of the fun things my brothers got to do at last...

Momma had a reputation of being very creative too. She did all sorts of crafts. She sold a lot of her crafts for extra income. It made it possible for her to buy Christmas gifts and of course more of the things she wanted. Daddy budgeted exactly one hundred dollars each year for my momma to spend on gifts for the five of us kids at Christmas time. That was about twenty bucks a piece on each one of us for gifts. You can imagine that we didn't get a lot of gifts. Even with the extra money my momma added towards gifts for us we might get around three at the most. That wouldn't have bothered me so much except that our friends always got an enormous amount of gifts for Christmas. One reason they got so many gifts was that their extended family all pitched in together to buy gifts for their families. Our family was never a close knit family. It seems that for some reason we were isolated pretty much from most of our extended families, and kept mostly to ourselves. For some strange reason daddy wanted it that way. Not getting lots of gifts for Christmas was a big deal for me back then. As I grew older it didn't matter much. I eventually realized the true meaning of Christmas and when I had children of my own, I made sure they knew too. I sort of went overboard with my first son James for the holidays, but everyone spoils their first child somewhat. After more sons came along I came to my senses. But not having the money to splurge anymore was a good enough reason.

I suppose the fruit doesn't fall far from the tree, because like daddy, I sort of stay to myself as an adult these days. As I look back over my days growing up in my parent's house, a lot of the crumbs from my parents table have actually made their way into my cornbread.

Chapter 2: About Cornbread

Oh boy do I remember my momma's cornbread! I am talking about lip smacking cornbread that you can eat. Just about every day my momma fixed cornbread with our dinner meal. On Sundays we usually had store bought rolls. But momma's cornbread was the bomb! Sometimes I came in the kitchen to watch her make it. She didn't measure the ingredients, but somehow the bread always turned out perfect. After the batter was mixed and stirred enough, she poured the batter slowly into the old seasoned iron skillet. She had put a big spoon of lard into the skillet beforehand and placed it into the oven to melt. I watched as the lard bubbled up around the sides of the batter. Momma would then take a big spoon and spread the hot melted lard around the edges of the batter. After that she would shake the pan gently to even out the batter, and place it in the oven to bake. Momma knew instinctively somehow just the right time to take a peek at the bread in the oven so it wouldn't sink in the middle. She would then close the oven and let the bread bake a few minutes more. Her cornbread came out a golden brown on top every time. She always spread some butter over the top of the bread to give it a buttery flavor when it was cut. I loved it when she would cut a small slice for me while it was piping hot. It was so good it made you want to slap yourself. I tried to duplicate how my momma made her bread when I was all grown up. But I was never able to make it taste as good as my momma's cornbread.

My daddy and momma weren't a very affectionate couple. At least I never knew them to be. I can count on one hand the times I ever saw them hug or kiss each other when I was a little girl growing up. My daddy gave me hugs when appropriate or the occasion called for it. I got a hug every time I ran to meet him when he was walking towards home after work. I coveted those hugs from my daddy. I recall very few hugs from my momma. I would watch the busses every day to see which one my daddy got off from so I could run to meet him. I did this just about every day until I was around nine years old. I don't recall either of my parents being affectionate to us very often. I believe they loved each other and my brothers and me. But I got the feeling there was some serious issues between my parents that they kept hidden. As I grew older I would learn about some of those hidden family issues.

My parents showed their love in other ways. For example my daddy was a great provider. He always managed to include family vacations and some fun things for us in his tight budget. I liked the family vacations the best. Every summer for as long as I can remember we went to visit my father's family in Dayton Ohio. My daddy would load as much food as possible, luggage with stuff for all of us, and all five of us children into the family car. My momma would do all the driving. Momma drove our old used green Studebaker car to make the trip in. I loved my family there in Ohio. We stayed for two weeks whenever we went. Just being away from Indianapolis was a real treat for me. I loved to sit at my grandma's feet as a little girl and listen to her stories. It was crowded in my grandma's big house with us and our aunts and uncles and cousins under one roof. But we all managed to squeeze into spaces to sleep and play. My daddy always seemed glad when it was time to head back home to his usual daily routine. But I hated to leave Ohio to go back to life as usual in Indianapolis.

Although my daddy's daily routine included working seven days a week. He did manage to squeeze a little time in for me and my brothers. There were the times spent with him on the front porch when he was finished reading the newspaper. I can still picture him sitting there on our front porch with his wide brim dusty gray hat sitting slightly to one side, wrapped in his favorite old grey sweater with the newspaper stretched out in front of him puffing on a cigar that hung from the corner of his mouth.

Our house was situated right across the street from Douglas Park. That made it nice for my daddy in the summers whenever local baseball teams came to play there. Sometimes he would take a folding chair over to the game. I could go with him if I wanted to. I really didn't care much for baseball, but I went occasionally just to spend more time with my daddy. My brothers and I got to spend time with daddy on the long walks with him to the store for groceries. We took turns. Those were special times for me with my daddy. On our trips to the grocery store daddy always stopped at the doughnut shop for fresh doughnuts. I loved the tantalizing smell and taste of the fresh yeast doughnuts as much as the small talk we made while walking.

On occasion daddy stopped on his way home from work and brought home to my momma a box of freshly roasted cashew nuts. My momma was especially nice to him when he brought her those cashew nuts home. She would make him one of his favorite desserts the next day. I liked it when my parents were nice to each other, because I got to eat some of their goodies and they seemed somehow to be really nicer to me and my brothers too.

Saturdays were special for me growing up in my parent's house too. My daddy gave all five of us twenty-five cents a piece on Saturdays to go to the local picture show. It cost ten cents to get in and the rest we spent on popcorn and candy. Momma always cooked hamburgers for us kids on Saturdays. We couldn't wait to get home to eat them. The show usually lasted about two hours. We were really hungry by the time it was over.

She usually made Kool-Aid for us to wash down the hamburgers with. We drank Kool-Aid every day. It was always spiced up with lemon juice the way my daddy liked it. My daddy had fresh milk delivered to our house every week. So we never ran out of Kool-Aid and we always had milk. That may be one reason why I probably got in the bad habit of drinking either of the two more than drinking just plain old water.

My daddy was a professional singer at one time. He had a high tenor singing voice. He never became famous or anything. But daddy was a pretty good singer. After meeting and falling in love with momma, He sacrificed his singing aspirations to become a business man. And he had attended a few years of business school prior to settling down and marrying my momma.

My momma was not well educated. She only went to the fifth grade in school. My daddy in many ways never let her forget that fact. Before my daddy and momma met each other momma was a teenage bride. She married at the age of fifteen and had two daughters from that marriage. My momma survived the abuse in that marriage and she eventually got a divorce. There was about twenty years between her first marriage and her marriage with my daddy.

Sometimes while my momma was doing house work she stopped to look in her cedar chest for a special record my daddy sang and recorded back then. He had dedicated a song on that record to me and my brothers.

She would rub the record on the bottom hem of her dress and place it carefully on the old "Victrola" record player to listen to. I loved it when momma played that record. For some reason she would always get a little starry- eyed when she played it. I don't remember whatever came of that record or record player for that matter. By the time I was school age momma never ever played that record ever again...

I spent a good portion of my growing up years in my parent's two houses on Martindale. I lived with them on Martindale until I was eighteen and joined the Army. The first house we lived in was in the twenty-three hundred block on Martindale next door to my mother's parents. Her parents owned the double. My daddy hated living there for some reason. When he had saved enough money to buy his own house we moved. The house daddy bought was in the twenty-seven hundred block on Martindale. I was around nine years old when we made that move. The new house was an old fixer-upper two story double. We lived in one half and my daddy rented the other half for income toward the monthly mortgage payment.

My brothers and I attended the same elementary school for all eight years of school. Daddy had planned it that way. But it was really boring and just ok for me. I was so sheltered growing up that I developed very little social skills. I lived in that stuffy close sheltered environment until I left home for the very first time. Don't get me wrong, I was blessed as a child to have two loving and caring parents. But in some ways their caring imposed tight controls that repressed my ability to make decisions. So when the time came for me to leave my parent's home to live my own life, I was an easy prey for all kinds of psychological miss-steps, sociopaths, and sexual predators.

My parents did their best to provide for me and my brothers. I am truly grateful for everything they gave me. But I always felt half empty growing up. And I always longed very much to be what I couldn't be; a "daughter of privilege"...

For as long as I can remember our bread and water was always sure in my parent's houses growing up. My daddy always had a way with words. So whenever daddy was speaking, as a rule we all listened. And he had this saying whenever he heard us complaining, "If you get hungry enough you'll eat sawdust". Thank God we never ate sawdust! And I thank God for the crumbs from His table and for my parent's half loaf...

Chapter 3: My Crumbs

I struggle with how to condense my story about my crumbs in this particular chapter. As I look back over my life it has truly been poignant, but yet even more so a rich and full one. There have been a myriad of twist and turns and bumps along the way. If I had thousands of books, I could fill them all from cover to cover with stuff both amazingly good and problematically bad. So I offer you just a peak into the mystery of a life less fulfilled but grateful for the crumbs that speak to the sum total of my life. For the lack of a better progression, in this book I will begin with my experience away from the secure shelter of my parent's home as an eighteen year old woman.

Turning eighteen was not met with much glee for me. There was no "Cotillion Ball" ushering me into high society. In fact there was not even a birthday party for me. It was in my mind just another day in my life. But before that day ended I was to learn how untrue that was. My daddy had his own set of meanings for my eighteenth birthday. It turns out that I was at the age of emancipation from daddy's stand point. With his blessings I could get married now or even live on my own. The cold hard truth was that I was no longer a tax write-off in regard to daddy's budget, but rather an un-welcomed liability. So marriage for me at that time would relieve him of any further responsibility for my care.

I had no real prospects for marriage lined up at my door, and even worse I had no job or career in sight. And to be quite honest College was not even an option. Then too, like so many other childhood dreams of mine, it too was just a dream. My daddy had the idea that college was definitely for my siblings. As college graduates they could be great providers for a wife someday. Don't get me wrong it's not like daddy was ready to throw me under the bus. He had high expectations for his princess. Daddy had sown seeds of hope into my life. Like the time he took me on my very first date. I remember it like it was just yesterday. Daddy had taken care to make our father daughter date special. I was just turning fifteen at the time. Daddy thought it was as good a time as any to inculcate me to the "Arts". By that time however I had already formed my own taste in music, culture and just about everything else. Although I applaud daddy for his efforts, looking back retrospect, I felt like daddy was trying to fit a square peg into a round hole. But at the time as a young girl, none of that stuff really mattered. I was daddy's princess and nothing was ever going to change that fact. It was the day of our date and I was so deliriously excited! The night before I had picked out my best dress to wear and the nice pair of shoes my Aunt Mamie had bought for me that year.

She had given me the money to purchase them because as she put it every young girl should have a good pair of dress shoes in her closet.

I fell in love with those shoes the first time I spotted them in the store window; and now they were mine. Lucky for me they still fit. I was in a growth spurt it seemed at that time and everything was getting either too short or too tight on me. My best dress however, still fit pretty well. It was a beautiful turquoise "Chemise" style dress. I slipped it gently over my head and let it cascade down around my slim frame. I made a few adjustments smoothing out the wrinkles with my hands so it fell just right over my hips. I looked at myself in the mirror one more time, lifted the hem of my dress to make a last minute tug at my silk stockings securing the knots and garters and slipped into my pretty sand toned flat shoes.

I bounced gleefully down the stairs and hurried into the living room where daddy was patiently waiting for me. I hardly noticed how handsome daddy looked because of the wide grin on his face and the spark of approval in his eyes when I entered the room. It was a magical glowing moment that only fathers and daughters share. The sound of daddy's dress shoes clicking on the pavement beside me gave me a sense of security as we headed for the bus stop. The evening sky was blurred by the misty rain that was hitting my cheeks as we walked briskly to get to the stop as the bus pulled up to let us board. Daddy was a frugal man, but tonight he was taking his princess on her very first date and he had sacked his budget. Daddy had purchased two VIP tickets for front row seats for the "Broadway" musical that was playing at the downtown Indiana Theatre. The marquee feature was "Porgy and Bess". It was a night to remember! I was lost in the exceptionally executed splendid acting and brilliance of the colorful scenes. I actually conceptualized the plot and energy of the story line and was captivated and touched by it all. It had opened me up to a world outside my humble existence even though if only for a night. It had sparked my imagination and nudged my longing for a life that I was not destined to have. The cold reality of the person I really was over shadowed the affects that whole experience at the age of fifteen might have brought to the table for me. And that experience was in the end merely a cruel reminder to me that I was not a daughter of privilege. But life goes on and at the age of eighteen I was still the princess my daddy always saw me as, nothing more and nothing less...

So my eighteenth birthday played out for me like a well-executed box office drama flick. Will anyone take the girl with the skinny legs? Nobody did; at least not yet. It would be three long years from my eighteenth birthday before I would for the first time marry...

I actually did emancipate myself from my parents when I turned eighteen. Can you believe it; I joined the Army! I had managed to graduate High School, but getting a job was next to impossible for me. So I went into the Army on the recommendation of a girlfriend. She and I were originally supposed to join together on the buddy program. It turns out she chickened out and didn't show up to be sworn in but I decided to go anyway...

Just as I was ill prepared for marriage when I turned eighteen, it was even more apparent in regard to being emancipated. The Army for me was the best of times and also the worst of times. The United States Army was a separate Army still in the year I joined (nineteen hundred and sixty-three). The women did Basic training separate from the men. But it was hardly a place for a young inexperienced woman like me.

The fact that I was a part of the Women's Army Auxiliary didn't make things any easier for me. Basic training was a holy terror. I was home sick most of the time during Basic.

And to make things worse I was a shy, puny, malnourished emotion wreck just waiting to happen. I literally had to gain twenty pounds before I passed the Physical for entrance into the Army. The real tragedy, however was that I was an easy mark for just about every type of sexual predator in the armed services as well.

I signed up for three years so that I could be guaranteed a spot in the Medical Corps. That was about the only thing that went as my recruiter promised. My Basic training was in Anniston Alabama. Back then the Army was integrated in regard to the races. But the state of Alabama was not. I was exposed to the "separate but equal" practices when it came time to go into town to buy dress pumps for our dress uniform. Back then "negro soldiers", had to go in town on a separate bus and at a different time from the white soldiers. I never knew shopping could get done so quickly! It was off the bus and into the store and back on the bus. So much for a tour of the city…

I managed to make it all the way through Basic training without a glitch. After a two week furlough to go home for Christmas I was transported by train to Ft. Sam Houston Texas for a twelve week school to become a Medical Corpsman.

I loved it there in Texas. I finally managed to learn how to fit in. That of course came with a price. You see to fit in I also learned how to drink alcohol and party with the in-crowd. I got really sloppy drunk for the first time the day I was supposed to leave Texas to go to my next assigned duty station in Maryland. I drank a lot that day to try and ease my grief. I had made friends there in Texas and really did not want to leave there. My friends had to literally pick me up and carry me to the bus and sit me in a seat on the bus that was leaving to go to the train station. I was high and crying most of the time on my trip to Maryland.

I finally arrived at my new Military post in Maryland. With my Military school in Texas and friends I made there all behind me, I decided to try and acclimate to my new surroundings.

The WAC Detachment where I lived was located in Maryland. It was situated just six miles from Washington D.C. where I was assigned to work. I worked as a Medical Corpsman for WRAMC (Walter Reed Army Medical Center). I really enjoyed my work there as a Medical Corpsman. But because I had no real social life there at first, it was boring. So to make things more interesting I began hanging out at the

NCO club. I did the club after work and most weekends. I soon found myself drinking again. It didn't matter to me about the drinking. All that mattered for me was that I fit in with the in-crowd. In addition to drinking I began to smoke cigarettes for the first time. My momma was a heavy smoker so it was a natural progression for me in my downward spiral.

But the worst possible thing that could ever happen to me while I was stationed in Maryland did. I was a victim of military sexual trauma. It happened to me twice while I was stationed in Maryland. In the first incidence I was assaulted by a male soldier who was also stationed there. In the second incidence an ex-soldier (veteran) assaulted and raped me. Prior to the assault he had gotten me pregnant. I knew he had a temper. But I was shocked by the fact that in a fit of jealous rage he could assault and rape me at gun point!

Back then the Army had different rules for handling unwed mothers. So I was not permitted to complete my remaining tour of duty. Just four months and six days short of my three year commitment in the Army, I was honorably discharged and headed back home to Indianapolis.

The traumatic events that played out for me in Maryland while in the military marked the beginning of my many years as a victim of abuse. From that time forward abuse became my familiar bedfellow for as long as I can remember…

The Army was truly more forgiving of the fact that I was an un-wed mother. There was a huge stigma back then placed on women who got pregnant out of wed-lock by society. And back then there was some real embarrassment for the families of un-wed mothers. In my case it was no exception. Even though I married my High School sweetheart, it was after the fact. I was still technically pregnant out of wed-lock prior to the marriage.

I gave birth to a bouncing baby boy in November of that same year after my discharge from the Army. At first my daddy took the news of my pregnancy very hard. I was his princess and I had let him down. He was bitter with me for a while and he made sure that I knew it. He went so far as to label my son a bastard child. As time went by he came around. Eventually, my first born son James became one of his favorite grandsons.

All around me crumbs were falling from my parents table, but I could barely gather them. I felt so dirty, unworthy and empty. Maybe it was the disappointment I could see in my father's eyes. Or maybe it was because the image I had of God had been so marred by the pain and hurt I felt deep down on the inside. I failed to thrive as a woman and a wife and mother during those years. I was a broken woman and I needed desperately to take hold of God's love for me.

My parent's house was not exactly where I wanted to be again at that time in my life. I hadn't planned for it to be that way. That was a big part of my problem. I had not really made any solid goals or realistic plans for my life while growing up. Because I had failed to plan, in essence I had by default planned to fail. So this time it was not just me alone living in my parent's house. My parent's house became for the time being an incubator for me and my very own personal dysfunctional family nucleus.

As I look back, I thank God that He didn't give up on me while I was going through. And that His crumbs were still available for me to make cornbread. It was up to me. From my parent's half loaf I still had enough crumbs to make a start. It wouldn't be easy. But somehow in my heart I knew it could be done. I would not despise my humble beginnings. My goal was to gather enough crumbs for myself to finally make my very own cornbread...

Chapter 4: Crumbs for My Sons

The loss of two sons has been very painful and truly sobering for me. My love and hunger for God is nothing short of miraculous. I actually was expected to do the blame game, and hate God if the Devil would have his way. Instead I cling unwaveringly to the promise of God that my latter end would be greater and better than my former years. I listen more intently now to the prophet of God who speaks a word over my life. I throw out any negative declarations and keep the positive. Recently a "word of Knowledge" was spoken over my life. It went like this:

> *"I am taking you through a process to heal your memories and bad experiences and I will bring peace and wholeness to your mind and life. This healing will affect the other areas of your life—areas where you have been sick in your body and areas where you have been insecure. As you let Me look at those old memories with you, you will realize I chose you just as you are and I ordained a special plan and destiny for your life that no one else can fulfil. Your past made you the person you are today. Your future will be brought to light as you see the self-confident person I will help you become. As you continue to look to me*

and sow seeds into my work, I will sow seeds into your
life and you will be healthy and whole."

God is truly turning my weeping into joy. And I'm trading in my ashes for beauty these days. I can see clearly now. The Son is beginning to shine brightly in my heart. The longing in my heart to be a "daughter of privilege" was my idea for me. It was never in the heart of God for me. God's ideal for me was and still is so much more. The Bible says so in **ICor.2:9 (TELB)** *But on the contrary, as the scripture says. What eye has not seen and ear has not heard and has not entered into the heart of man, [all that] God has prepared (made and keeps ready) for those who love Him [who hold Him in affectionate reverence, promptly obeying Him and gratefully recognizing the benefits He has bestowed].*

So I won't take anything for my journey now. My life is now for certain hid in Christ Jesus. Now that I know for myself that Christ Jesus lives in me, no demon in hell can separate me from His love! The journey in this chapter and the next two chapters is for all the mothers and fathers who have lost children to drugs or some catastrophic illness or even death. I have been transparent in the hopes that it will perhaps bring you comfort and hope in some meaningful way...

It was a day that began as so many did for me after the loss of my sons. It may have been too early still for me to get up after another sleepless night of remembering. I was preparing myself mentally to face another day without James and William. I thanked God for loving me and for the time I had spent with my sons when they were alive. And then I turned over on my back and just laid there quiet and still. The phrase "sons of thunder" flashed through my mind as I lay there. I mussed over the meaning. I wrestled with the idea that perhaps it could have some religious or prophetic import. I began to correlate the phrase with those unsettling memories of my two sons James and William. In some crazy way it spoke to the manner in which they entered into my life and exited. And I began to piece together the string of events that describes that turbulent season in my life.

The months and years preceding the births and deaths of my sons James and William remind me of being in a fierce storm. At times I was tossed about to and fro by the billows and waves of life. There were times when the breakers dashed and lightening flashed over my life relentlessly. Then there were the days that I simply weathered the storm. The torrential waters of despair and adversity might have swallowed me up had it not been for God… God has always and continues to be my shelter in the time of storm. It was during the times that God stilled the storms in my life that I gathered enough crumbs from His table for my two sons.

Chapter 5: Crumbs for William

Sunrise: December 17, 1974   *Sunset*: February 13, 2004

I became pregnant too soon after the birth of my first son James. Because my body was not prepared to carry another baby to term I experienced what is called a spontaneous abortion. It is also known as miscarriage. I was about three and a half months pregnant when I aborted the fetes. To make matters worse it happened on my son James very first birthday. I had absolutely no medical insurance when this occurred. I was taken by ambulance to the General Hospital for my care. Because my care was substandard at this particular hospital, I developed an infection in my fallopian tubes. Heavy scaring also developed in both tubes. I was unable to get pregnant for seven years following that miscarriage. For me those seven years seemed like twenty.

I went into a deep depression during those years. I could barely look at a pregnant woman back then. Even newborn babies had an effect on me. I was constantly pressured by my husband to have his biological child. With each passing month I failed to get pregnant I sank further and further into despair. He truly loved James, but he very much wanted a child he fathered too. I became so frustrated that I had to take medicine for stress and insomnia. I prayed and prayed and prayed and prayed to God to open my womb again. It seemed that God hadn't heard my prayers as the years went by without the desired results.

I was enrolled in Modelling School and working a part-time job at a major department store when I finally learned I was pregnant. I was thrilled! To my dismay my husband was not. My marriage was falling apart at the seams, and already in trouble by the time I finally became pregnant with William. Not long after William was born in 1974, my husband and I separated. In 1977 some three years later, we divorced.

William was around fourteen months old when I attended a religious meeting and dedicated him to God. At William's dedication, I decided to also re-dedicate my life to God. It was my way of showing God my gratitude for blessing me with William. I had already dedicated my son James to God years earlier when he was around two months old.

As time passed, it became very clear to me that the devil was angry with me. He was angry about my determination to bring up my sons to fear God, and my commitment to honor God. From that day forward the devil launched an all-out, full scale attack on me and my two sons James and William. The devil wanted to kill all three of us by any means possible.

My son William met his untimely death at the age of twenty nine in Denver Colorado. He died in a house fire that was set intentionally. He was knocked unconscious sprinkled with a flammable liquid and set on fire. William's body was burned beyond recognition. He was a "John Doe" for two weeks until a DNA test verified that the body was him.

When I learned about his death I was working in South Korea as a volunteer Missionary. I was devastated by the news. My first reaction was that of dismay. I remember a terrible anguish that is difficult to describe. The first few hours were the worst for me. I felt like my stomach was going to explode from the intense twisted churning I felt deep down on the inside. I was listless and pitiful. And I felt like a sick helpless puppy dog. I remember crying until my cries were swallowed up into a whimper. I want to thank the Brown family (Robert and Tamara) for literally taking me under their wings and into their home for the night. Around three in the morning God began to minister to me and console me. He gave me three scripture texts that spoke to my grief that I will cherish forever.

The first one was II Corinthians 5:1 (NIV):

"Now we know that if the earthly tent we live in is destroyed, we have a building from God, an eternal house in heaven not built by human hands."

The second one was Psalms 84:3 (NIV):

"Even the sparrow has found a home, and the swallow a nest for herself, where she may have her young- a place near your alter, O Lord Almighty, my King and my God."

The third one was Jeremiah 31:15, 16, 17 (TCW):

"I heard a voice in Ramah near the tomb of Rachel, a voice of mourning and bitter weeping. The mothers in Israel are weeping for their children who were killed. They refuse to be comforted

because their young ones have been taken captives to Babylon. But stop your crying and wipe your tears. Everything you have done for your children will not go unrewarded. I will bring them back from death and from the land of the enemy. There is hope for you, O Israel, in the Lord your God. Your children will return home. They will come back to their own country. I the Lord have spoken."

I cling each day to the blessed hope I have indeed in God. How William ended up in a house fire that took his life is a painful journey that began for him at the tender age of twelve years old. That was the first time he decided to experiment with recreational drugs. I was not aware of this until years later when he was an adult.

I truly tried to protect William as a parent. But with each failed marriage, I became this struggling single parent and who had to work for much of my son's growing up years. I had very little help from the absent parent in terms of William's emotional well-being and his day to day care. He and his brother James were basically "latch key" kids.

When I saw red flags in William's behavior I immediately notified the Social Services. Their response amounted to brushing my concerns off by attributing them to simple childhood antics. They insisted that William would grow out of it. So, the system at that point truly failed both me and William.

By the time I realized that William had serious problems and that he was actually an addict it was too late! He was a youth by then with lots of anger issues and no trust in the system that was supposed to be there for us. William ended up being a part of the system that failed him. He was in and out of jail, and in and out of a cycle of drug treatment and relapse from the time he was fourteen years old until his death.

To complicate matters William also had a mental illness. William was clinically diagnosed with schizophrenia as a young adult, after an episode that landed him in the hospital. William had displayed strange behavior sometimes as a small child growing up. What I thought was just him messing around was actually undiagnosed schizophrenia. Unfortunately, like so many other things going on with William as a child, he had managed to hide it from me and those close to him.

William did share with his older brother James that the recreational drugs (Crack Cocaine was his drug of choice) actually quieted the voices in his head. William self-medicated himself with recreational drugs. He simply could not trust the system enough to allow them to treat his illness with traditional medications. The recreational drugs became William's best friend, but also his worst enemy over time.

While the drugs worked to still the voices in his head, William could not hold a job very long while doing drugs. He would stop taking the drugs in order to work. But, it was not very long before the voices would return to taunt William.

William was always in a catch twenty-two. William's drug habit and mental illness caused him to do things for which he had many regrets. But William never stopped trying to change his plight. He wanted desperately to work and have a good life. He wanted to become something in life.

After finally earning his GED for High School, William filled out forms that would enable him to get a College education. His acceptance papers for college arrived just a few weeks after his death.

William was never alone in his struggles, although at times I'm sure he might have felt that way. Those who truly loved him were always there for him. He wanted to trust people, but his illness made that nearly impossible. He even had difficulty believing that I loved him. I will always remember that tender moment that William confided in me that he was convinced at last that I really loved him. That revelation came after he attempted to embarrass me in a church meeting I was attending one day. He was acting out his anger against me by walking over pews filled with worshipers during the service. He was taken out of the sanctuary that day by some deacons on duty to a room in the basement. He thought I would be really angry with him for what he had done. I could have been, but I was more hurt than anything. God impressed me to go to my son at once and just stroke him and to tell him that I love him. It worked! William never tried to embarrass or hurt me in public from that day on. In fact, he always went out of his way to show me that he loved me.

William was raised in church and attended church school up to the eighth grade before drugs changed his life forever. I truly believe that his sense of God kept him from being eternally lost. He was often confused with what was truth. It was those voices that kept him confused. He would be swayed by various religious people in his quest for truth. He was attracted to several religious denominations at any given time. Although William was baptized as a young boy, he decided to be re-baptized as a young man at the age of twenty-five. The age of twenty-five seemed to be a turning point in William's life. He became a proud father of a son at that age. Perhaps that was the driving force in his life at that point that kept him from giving up on life completely. He still did drugs, but he was more determined than ever to make a better life for his son.

It would be four long years of struggling with drugs and his illness before William bottomed out.

I was in South Korea when I got the call from William that I had prayed and longed for. William expressed to me that he was unhappy with the way his life had turned out and wanted to try to make things right. He wanted to return to Colorado to finish his probation requirements, get a job, and enroll in College once that was done. It was something in his voice that let me know he was serious this time.

He wanted to know what I thought. I let him know that what he was proposing was great, but the decision to complete his probation would have to be his decision.

In 2003, William did return to Denver Colorado to complete his probation. He was a free man later that same year. The sad thing was that William could not free himself from the drugs and the voices. In December of 2003, William turned twenty-nine years old. Not long after, he relapsed and was back out on the streets of Denver. His earthly end was met in his apartment.

Among his personal effects was a journal that William had kept prior to his death. In that journal William said that he regretted the day he ever took that first drug as a twelve year old boy. He expressed that he wanted something better for his son. And William wrote a short prayer to God asking Him to bless and watch over his son Eljin, and to keep him safe from drugs.

William entered his blessed rest on Friday the thirteenth of February. I believe that God in His mercy did what was best for William. You see I had cried out to God for William about two months prior to his death. And I gave William back to God permanently. I asked God to either heal him completely or put him out of his misery. The devil also heard my prayer that day.

In my mind, this is why William died so tragically! But God gave me peace in my heart. He let me know that William will be among the redeemed of the earth when Jesus comes again. God gave me this assurance in such a very special way.

While I was still working in South Korea as a Missionary, my son James sent me an e-mail valentine from the states. It was the popular scripture text John 3:16. In the caption on the e-mail it read, "The Greatest Valentine in the World". I received the e-mail on Friday the Thirteenth the same day my son William was killed.

I truly believe William on the day when the trumpet shall sound will hear his name and come forth and be changed from his corruptible state into an in-corruptible being in a twinkling of an eye. And he will be with Jesus throughout the ceaseless eons of eternity.

Now, I celebrate William's life in Christ Jesus even though I mourn his death. Each new day is a reminder to me of how much God truly loves William. And oh how I long for that blessed resurrection morn! William is finally free! His son Eljin lives with his mother and sister in Texas. I don't see much of him these days. I pray for Eljin and his family daily.

My hope and prayer for all those William left behind to mourn his death is that his death not be in vain. That somehow his life struggles and experiences will speak to the hearts of those who can learn from them.

His poems and writings are just a sample of how talented he was in life in spite of his struggles. I hope you enjoy them as much as I did compiling them and editing them for you.

Chapter 6: Crumbs for James

Sunrise: November 5, 1966   *Sunset*: May 6, 2008

My first born son James…

What can I say about James that truly captures the essence of who he was to me? James grew up and left my household when he was eighteen. Much of what happened in his life after that is left to speculation. We loved each other very much. There were lots of happy reunions and a mixture of sad good-byes along the way. Much to my regret because of my own troubles and William's neediness as a child growing up in my household, not a lot of energy was left to focus much my attention toward James. He sort of had to just grow up!

So I'll begin his story a few months before I became pregnant with him...

I actually dreamed I was going to be pregnant with James before it ever happened. I was still in the military at the time of my dream. The last thing I had ever planned to do back then was to get pregnant. I had actually planned to get out of the service a single carefree woman with no real responsibilities. I had this crazy idea that I would travel a lot and party my life away. But one day as I was sleeping in my barracks I saw a vision of me with a soldier and then a vision of a baby boy came before my eyes. It was so real that I awoke in a state of frantic anxiety and panic. And I made a vow to myself to stay clear of all potential romantic relationships with soldiers. It worked for a while...

I was at a house party off base when I met my waterloo. I thought it was safe to mingle at the party because there were no men there in uniform. The man I began conversing with seemed much older and didn't act at all like a soldier to me. At least not like the soldiers I knew on base. We danced a lot together, and I decided I wanted to get to know him more. It turned out the party was actually at his house. So he asked me to stay after the party to spend time with him. I had no intention of letting that happen. But, I was drinking heavy and began to let my guard down as the night progressed. At that point, I was depending on the friends I came with to keep an eye out for me. At some point, I realized they had left me with my new acquaintance.

Before I realized how I got there, I was totally alone with him in his bed. The rest is history...

I was right technically to think he was not a soldier, but I had not considered that he could be a veteran. He had actually served in the Army! So my dream came true to the letter. I had known my son James's father exactly one month before I got pregnant. I was furious with him! I felt stupid and betrayed. I even thought of ending my life. One of my girlfriends convinced me that suicide was not the solution.

There were a lot of things I didn't know about the man I got pregnant by. Aside from the fact he was a veteran, I learned that he was also married and separated from his wife. He also had a son with his wife and they lived just across town. According to him, he was separated from his wife because she had messed around on him with another man. He had caught them together, and beat her up badly. He was still pretty much angry with her when he and I met.

What I didn't know was that he was a dangerous man to be with. He had a violent temper which I found out about the hard way. One day in a violent rage he turned on me because he thought I was messing around with his cousin. Before I could convince him that was not true, he attacked me. He beat me repeatedly with his fist and held a gun to my temple and forced me to have sex with him at gun point! I thought he was actually going to pull the trigger. After that horrific traumatic experience, I left him and was discharged from the military. I got as far away from him as I could. And thank God, I never saw him again. My son James passed away never meeting his biological father. I think it was perhaps better that way. James did, however, experience the love of a father through my first husband.

As I look back over my life, I regret the fact that my second marriage was not a fit for my son James. It had all of the classic pitfalls of a blended family. My second husband and I weren't really ready to take on the challenges we were faced with. There was simply too much baggage to deal with. I probably would have never married him had it not been for my mother and pressure from my church. I was living in sin with my second husband prior to marrying him—the practice commonly known as shacking.

A lot of things were broken in my second marriage, and they could not be fixed. For example, my son James and his stepfather did not get along. Their disdain for each other came to a head when James was around seventeen years old. Words were exchanged and tempers flared. It got physical sometimes as well. Finally James got fed up and moved out without giving me any warning. He just cleaned out his closet and drawers one day while I was at work. I was so heartbroken that I cried uncontrollably. The Sabbath after it happened, I went to church a broken mother. When it was prayer time I went up to the front for special prayer, and I poured out my tears to God. No words would come. God saw my tears and heard my heart pleas for my son. That next day my son came back home.

I wanted to make things better for my son when he came back, but I couldn't. He left again for good some months later when he turned eighteen. This time he told me he was moving out. That would be the last time for many years that my son James and I would be a part of the same household...

Twenty-two years passed before my son James and I would be in the same household again. A lot happened in our lives during that long separation. One thing never changed during those years, the love of a mother for her son and the love of a son for his mother. There are many happy memories of things we did when we all came together as a family on holidays and special occasions. I always kept in touch with my son

James and we talked on the phone often. But, our lives took different paths for the most part. I was busy with the responsibility of providing for his younger brother William and the two sons that were born after William, Juan and Michael. My son James was busy with his own life. He was pursuing his dreams for a promising career and family of his own someday.

I had high hopes for my first born son James. I saw greatness in him and his brothers. I always told each of them that they could be someone great in life. For James, I saw a future perhaps in Government. His life was heading in that direction when I left Indianapolis to enroll in a four year college. James declined my offer for him to go with us. The year was nineteen hundred and eighty-eight. It was the fall season of that year when I left Indianapolis.

While I was a student at Oakwood College, my son James was actually realizing some of his dreams. He was popular with the honeys, and had a perspective wife picked out. At least the list was down to about two. He was also making a great income for himself. By the time I transferred to another College, Andrews University, he was well on his way to being able to provide for a wife comfortably.

One day, he called me and asked me the question I had been expecting. He was ready to settle down and make plans with the woman he would marry. He asked me which of his two choices of women would be the right one for him. I gave him some advice and told him the choice would have to be his alone.

My son did choose the one he felt was right for him and began to plan his future around her. They even picked out a house in an up-scale neighborhood. From the outside looking in things were going well and as planned. But, there were forces at work in this life that sought to destroy everything good and beautiful. The devil had devised a plan that would change the course of my son's life forever in the blink of an eye.

I was living in Denver Colorado when I got the phone call from my son's fiancé. I had moved to Denver in nineteen hundred and ninety-six after graduating the Theological Seminary in Michigan. I was invited to Denver to do a year Chaplain Residency and to also complete the remaining requirements that year to become a Chaplain. The year-long program was almost over. I was at home when the call came. I will never forget that phone call.

She said that my son was in the hospital and in serious condition from a Motorcycle accident. The news stunned me so bad that I was speechless for a moment. I had just talked to my son that week, and he was excited that he would be able to buy another motorcycle. It was an upgrade from the one he had at the time.

I slept very little that night after the bad news about my son. I had very little income from my work at the hospital. So, I had resigned myself to the fact that I would not be able to purchase a ticket to go to the bedside of my son in Indianapolis.

I could barely bring myself to face people I worked with the next day. I didn't know how on earth I was going to be there for the patients I would visit that day. It was while I was in the conference room with my supervisor and co-workers that I broke down. I shared with them what had happened to my son. The tears ran down my cheeks and my voice was a bumbling mess. I will never forget what happened next! I know there must be a God in heaven who loves me. To my surprise I was told by my supervisor to arrange for the next flight leaving for Indianapolis, so I could be there with my son. All of the cost was being taken care of by the hospital I worked for.

I want to take a commercial break here to say that God's pay is good. Man can't pay us what God has already paid on Calvary! For loving us there is no charge.

When I arrived in Indianapolis, my son had been moved from intensive care to a room. He was still pretty messed up from the accident. I could tell that he was in a lot of pain. The medical staff had induced a semi-coma to keep him as calm as possible. He recognized me but was barely able to talk. His chin had been injured and a metal plate inserted to replace the damaged part. They were still running test on him and had the results of a few. His blood alcohol level was high when he was admitted, and they wanted to know his drinking habits. His father seemed to be in denial, but I had known for some time it was not good.

I told the doctors that he drank almost every day and might go into DTs. Just as I had predicted, that is what happened next. He had a seizure, then suffered a stroke from complications of alcohol withdrawal in his system that day. It left him paralyzed on his left side and some moderate brain damage. To make things worse, he was also diagnosed with a very serious heart disease. From an x-ray that was taken of his chest the doctors discovered that James had splitting around the aortic valve of his heart. The condition is known as Marfan syndrome. James would have to have heart surgery the next day to fix the valve and prevent it from splitting further. If the valve had split all the way around James would have died instantly from that. While the accident was terrible, we would have never known about the heart valve if it were not for the accident.

The additional complications overwhelmed me for a moment. It looked bad, but I believed God was going to work everything out for the good. I slept in the hospital all that night prior to his surgery. I prayed fervently in between thoughts of my son and my bouts of broken sleep.

God spared my son's life that day of the accident. He didn't let my son die from the heart disease, and the surgery went well. But, in the years after those trying days in the hospital James would have to undergo two more heart surgeries. The damage fallout from the entire physical trauma left my son total and permanently disabled for the rest of his life at the age of thirty years old.

There are no words to adequately describe how I was hurting for my son. From the day I got the terrible news of his accident forward I began to grieve for my son James and what might have been. By the time James was discharged from the hospital he had lost his health, his fiancé, his ability to get wealth and his promising future. But, it was truly a miracle that James was alive and things in his life were as well as they were.

As I look back, perhaps there were things that I could have done to make life better for him. But my son was still a young man and too full of pride. He tried to make his life as normal for himself as he knew how. Getting counseling or help from a support group was not for him he thought. Being pampered by his mother was not an option either. James was thirty years old when he had his accident. In James' mind he was still that healthy twenty nine year old man he was the year prior to his accident. He lived out the remainder of his life in that frame of mind. After the doctors in Indianapolis had done all they could for my son, his condition began deteriorating rapidly. I thought more than once that it was over for him. But, God still had a plan for James filled with hope and a future.

It's time for another commercial break. We each may find ourselves in a situation like James on any given day. We might even be in a situation right now that is devastating and life threatening. God allows us to go through things sometimes so He can bring us out. No matter what it seems like or how bad it is, God loves us too much to leave us there. Before the situation or problem ever gets to us it has to go through Jesus. And Jesus will not allow the enemy to put upon us more than we can bear.

Although I grieved my son's diminished quality of life, I was still grateful to God that he was still alive. It was nothing but a miracle that my son did not die that fateful day of his accident. The sun was beaming brightly in the afternoon sky. It was turning out to be another hot sunny day as usual. James had been visiting with his friend Wendell on that particular afternoon. He intended to show him the new motorcycle he had just purchased that same morning. It was a larger cycle than the one he had traded in. It was also a newer model.

James had not really tested it out for breaking speed and other safety features. He didn't even have his protective gear on for some reason. While he was visiting Wendell he heard motorcycle engines just around the corner from them and decided to ride his new cycle around there. When he got there he discovered they were racing their cycles. He made a decision to race his new cycle. I am sure that decision went against his better judgment.

James had taken the driving course for motorcycles. He knew he was taking a risk racing his new cycle because he was not familiar with the breaking speed. But, James decided to race it anyhow. He fired his cycle up, and began to press on the gas. Before he knew it, he was a speeding down the block. In a matter of seconds, he had reached a busy intersection. He was speeding too fast to either slow the cycle down or break fast enough to keep from going across the intersection which contained oncoming cars.

In a panic he hit the motorcycle's breaks, but it was too late. He was flipped into the air and crash landed head first onto a wire fence on the other side of the intersection, and landed on the grass. The fence was on a church property. He barely missed a car that was in the intersection as he was sliding across it. Eye witnesses gasped it terror at what they saw. They were sure my son was killed because the car was travelling through the intersection at the very same time my son was on his cycle going through the intersection. They described it as something out of a science fiction movie. It looked to them like the car was so close that it actually passed through my son on his cycle as it kept going. The church fence actually prevented my son from breaking his neck. All I can say is but God...

Through the tragedy in my son James' life, I have come to know that God truly has a plan and purpose for each one of us. I was busy trying to micro manage the remainder of my son's life by trying to make things happen or not happen in my own power. God let me map out my plans and then He began to show me His. I decided that God knows best!

This is how God began to work His plan. I received information about a position that was opening up at a Women's Shelter in Michigan from a friend of the family Cynthia Prime. Living in Michigan again would put me closer to Indianapolis and to my son James. The Director of the shelter offered me the position. I accepted her offer, and moved to Michigan in the year 2YK (Two- thousand). That year was pivotal in the rebuilding my relationship with my son James...

Now getting back to what happened in Denver. One day while sitting in church, I thought about all four of my sons and their baptisms. All four were baptized as young boys under the age of eleven years old. They had all attended church school for a portion of that time. To my knowledge, only one was re-baptized as a young adult. That was William. James may have done so, but I don't recall if he did. The thing that really stuck out in my mind was that God had directed me to get re-baptized again in 2004 upon my return from South Korea. It just so happened that I was living in my son James' household in Denver when God gave me the directive. My son James is among those who were witnesses to that re-baptism. I have to believe that somehow God meant that baptism to bring healing for me, but also for James as well. James had witnessed as a child some of my improprieties as a single woman. And some things about me were hidden away privately that nobody knew but me and God. On the outside I was a good Christian woman. But, on the inside I was a hypocrite. One of the hidden iniquities of mine was my dabbling in soft porn. I am sharing this now because I want to perhaps help some other Christian women who may be travelling down that same path. I did not understand why God insisted on my re-baptism. I had already made a vow to myself and to God to denounce all sexual sin in my life. But, I was not yet free of some of the fallout from it. I felt in my heart it was wrong, but I didn't have the power in me to overcome this perverted behavior. It was not until I obeyed God, and was re-baptized that I was at last set free of the desire for it. I thank God for delivering me from myself.

God revealed to me prior to my son James's death that he had a very serious addiction to pornography and it was a diabolical stronghold. This stronghold prevented James from being very spiritual and in an intimate relationship with God. It was choking the spiritual life out of him. In order for me to help my son, God had to first heal me. My re-baptism and my changed life while in my son's household were crucial to my influence upon my son's walk with God.

I want to take a short commercial break right here. I am so grateful to God that when He found me in sin He loved me too much to leave me there. I'm so glad too that God's grace and mercy reached out and grabbed me when I was in the military. My foolish plan was to roam from state to state aimlessly. But thanks to God, He had a better plan for my life!

James' move to Denver Colorado was not an easy one for him. He had lots of deep roots that went back to his birth in Indianapolis. I believe my son knew that his time remaining was not long. He had experienced a mother's love when I visited him in Indianapolis while I was working at the Shelter in Michigan. This helped him to realize he wanted to be where I was.

Although the doctors in Indianapolis had given up on him after having done all they could do for him, James still had hope. He still took the prescribed medicines, and went for check-ups. In the months prior to his death he still clung to that hope. But he expressed that he was so tired of all the medical procedures to prolong his life and the medications.

It was before his move to Denver, while he was still in Indianapolis, and at the point when I thought I was about to lose my son that I decided to have a serious mother son talk with him. I went way back to his childhood and began to apologize for all the times that I failed him. I expressed my sorrow for not being able to protect him while I was at work during the day from things that might have happened to him. I learned that one of those "things" was his exposure to pornography as a young boy by a person of trust. I begged for his forgiveness for the trauma he experienced while I was in dysfunctional toxic relationships with the men in my life.

At first, this purging of my soul was met with a haunting silence. But, he finally expressed that he understood. He told me that I was forgiven. From that moment forward, I vowed that I would never again allow myself to be in another toxic dysfunctional relationship. My silent prayer to God at that time was that he would give me another chance to make it right for me and my sons. I asked God to bring me together with the right man who would work together with me to model a healthy relationship before my sons. It would be many long years before God would answer my prayers...

When my son finally moved to Denver Colorado in two thousand and four, He began to see a positive change in his life. Moving to Denver was the best decision he could have ever made. James received the best medical care possible. He was able to take advantage of some of the best heart and brain injury specialists in the country. Being around his brothers and me gave him a reason to thrive. His overall health improved greatly. It seemed that James was happy and reasonably content.

When I moved into James' apartment in Denver after returning to the States from South Korea, it was the first time since his teen years that I was exposed to his personality and lifestyle choices. The real James was on pass and review. Of course, he got to know some of my idiosyncrasies too. It was during this time I became more aware of James' excessive interest in pornography. My first real clue was when I sat down at his computer and saw his screen saver. It was a picture of a woman's naked chest with her bust exposed. Her bust measurement would've made Dolly Pardon blush! In his bedroom was a poster pic of Janet Jackson with ... you guessed it. Her bust was exposed also.

I am a woman, but I was actually offended by the screen saver. After expressing to my son my concerns he changed the screen saver.

I didn't have to be in his bedroom, so the Janet Jackson picture stayed there. He just turned the picture over so I wouldn't see it if I needed to be in his room for any reason. He tried to please me by changing his screen saver, but he really had no problem with it being there. I learned later that what I saw initially was just the tip of the iceberg.

Whenever I used the computer after my son, I noticed lots of pop-ups of porn sites. One day he forgot to clear his mailbox and there was a vulgar porn page about mothers with numerous lewd remarks. It was like right in my face type of trash. That was a huge red flag for me! I began an all-out campaign against this sexual perversion that was dominating so much of my son's time and attention. That year, I made a financial sacrifice to make sure he could attend a Men's Retreat sponsored by our church. I was prepared to go into the enemy's camp if necessary to secure my son's freedom from this insidious vice.

The more I prayed for James, the more the enemy began to turn up the heat. The Devil began an all-out brutal attack on my son's health. Once again as it did in Indianapolis, my son's health began to decline again significantly. By the latter part of two thousand and seven it was apparent. I was so used to my son being able to do most things for himself that I had barely noticed his decline. It was gradual at first. By February of the next year everything began to surface again in regard to James' heart condition. But, I was totally not prepared for what happened that month.

The day started off fairly normal. I had spoken briefly with James that February morning before he left the house for a court matter. It was just small talk. He had not asked me to go with him to court because I had not been feeling well at the time. The phone rang about two hours later. I picked up the phone, and my son was on the other end. He gave me some incredibly disturbing news. It turned out that he had actually taken ill in the courtroom and was rushed by ambulance to a nearby hospital with severe abdominal pain. Upon examination the doctors detected a hernia that was life threatening and blocking his intestines. They wanted to do emergency surgery.

As my hand went limp around the phone, my head began to spin, and my mind went back to my son William and his horrific death. It was a bad memory for me. In the month of February two thousand four my son William was killed. And now my son James was at deaths door once again, and I felt helpless to make it go away. With a gaping black hole of panic building inside of me, like that of a worried silly desperate mother I belted out, 'But what about your heart condition?' And I dropped the phone, and lowered myself in slow motion as I reached in back of me for the frame of the large brown couch next to the wall. My trembling frame fell onto the soft pillow beneath me. I lifted the phone back up to my ear. The weight of the cold black phone in my hand startled me as my son's voice broke the silence, "Yes". Unable to manage any more coherent meaningful words, I told my son that I was on my way there.

I knew my son was not ready spiritually to meet Jesus in peace. I also knew that I was not ready to let him go. My mind was beginning to scramble and go into stress mode. I didn't have a car to get to the hospital, and no money to pay for a taxi cab. My heart began to sink into the pit of my stomach. I couldn't even utter a prayer. I called my closest friend Trish and blurted out to her that my son James is being prepared for emergency surgery. She didn't ask if I needed a ride to the hospital she just said I'm on my way.

I wasn't sure if we would arrive at the hospital before the doctors took my son into surgery, so I began to ask God to not let him die without having made his peace with Him. I began to plead with God to save my son. I tried to picture in my mind what my son was going through. My imagination was running wild. What if I'm too late!

We did arrive too late for me to pray with my son. They had taken him into surgery just about ten minutes before we arrived. The hospital staff instructed us to go into the waiting room. I can't adequately describe my feeling of sheer panic mixed with tears and unutterable pleas to God for my son's life. It seemed like I was waiting an eternity when a doctor finally came into the waiting room. I tried to read his face but couldn't. He immediately assured me my son was still alive. What he said next caused me to gasp.

My son's heart had stopped on the operating table and they had to stop the surgery to try to revive him and bring him back to life. No one can ever tell me that my God does not hear and answer prayer. God had heard my pleas for my son and in His mercy brought him back to me. At least that was true for the time being...

We couldn't go in to see James until they had cleaned him up and changed his bed sheets. It seemed like another eternity had passed when the staff nurse took us at last in to see my son. He was drowsy from the meds they gave him to keep his heart quiet and resting. The first thing I asked him was did he know that he had technically died on the operating table, was resuscitated, and had come back to life. He nodded yes. But, his expression didn't seem to grasp the gravity of the miracle that God had performed in his behalf. For the most part, it seemed he was oblivious to his surroundings as well. He was in no way out of the woods.

The doctors had explained to me just how critical my son's condition really was. If he did not have the surgery he would die from the hernia. If he had the surgery, chances are that he would not make it through the surgery. In other words, the doctors had little hope that my son would survive either way. The doctors may have given up, but I was not going to let go until God blessed me with an assurance of my son's salvation. From that moment on, I never ceased to pray for the salvation of my son.

The heart doctors and surgery team had devised a plan of action for the next day. They would use a special monitor for his blood pressure while he was undergoing the surgery on his hernia so his pressure wouldn't drop too quickly again. Now, all they would need was my son's consent to do the surgery. I was standing at my son's bed side when the doctors came to tell him their plan. They explained to my son that his chances of survival with the surgery were slim to none. And if they didn't do the surgery at all he would probably die from the hernia within a few days.

As I looked at my son the expression on his face was not like any I had ever seen before. It was a look of helplessness mixed with hopelessness and sheer fear. It was so unsettling and sobering for me that I had to look the other way. After what seemed like an eternity had passed my son requested that they perform the surgery. I had never witnessed my son cry before. This situation would not be any different. His eyes did tear up, but no tears fell that day. It was as though he wanted to cry but was fighting hard not to.

The fact that my son requested the surgery let me know that he was not ready to give up. It let me know also he was not ready to die. My son wanted another chance, and God granted him just that. My son didn't live a long time after his surgery. The surgery was in February of two thousand and eight and my son passed in May of that same year. But, it was long enough for God to save him.

I stayed at the hospital all that night to the next morning of my son's scheduled surgery. The surgery waiting room had begun to fill up on that day with people. My sons Juan and Michael, and my close friend Trish arrived to wait with me. I had slept little the night before, and was a basket case by the time they arrived. I felt like I was in the Twilight Zone.

Lots of people were praying for my son's surgery to be a success. My prayer to God was for God to save my son. I prayed that particular way because I did not have peace in my heart that my son was at peace with God yet. Even if my son made it through the surgery, if he was not at peace with God, his very soul could be lost.

As I prayed for my son's salvation, I also asked God to show me what was preventing my son from being at peace with Him. God revealed to me that it was my son's addiction to pornography that was preventing him from connecting to God, and that I needed to make my son aware of this. I asked God how I was to proceed and to word my mouth. I was impressed to write my son a letter because he would receive the counsel from God more readily that way. With the guidance of the Holy Spirit, I penned a letter revealing God's love and grace for him that I believe made all the difference.

I did not witness any drastic changes in my son, but I detected an inner peace about him. He even agreed to take a Bible study from me. I was totally surprised that he accepted. We had completed about eight studies in a series of thirteen before his health took a serious turn for the worse. He would sit quietly and listen at a distance whenever my Throne Room small group met and we were studying the topic of the Holy Spirit. The real blessing was that my son agreed to be anointed by our Pastor two days prior to his peaceful death.

I believe that anointing finally broke the yoke of sexual sin that had held my son bound for years. Although he was confined to a wheel chair, James requested that we take him to church before he passed. He really enjoyed his last church service with me and his brother Juan.

I was at peace with my son's death because my son had found his place in God's kingdom and his salvation through Christ Jesus. My son passed away just days prior to Mother's Day. I can't tell you how hard that was for me. Other special days bothered me greatly that first year of his death.

As a Chaplain I learned how to deal with other people's grief. But going through my own has been horrendous for me at times. No amount of text book knowledge can ever prepare you for your own personal grief. I now grieve the loss of two precious sons. I'm afraid I don't do my own grief very well. In fact, when William died I had to get some professional help to deal with it. From my training as a Chaplain, I learned that while all grief is the same everyone's experience with grief is different. I know that to be a fact. I grieve differently for each of my two sons.

Some time ago, I went through a class that dealt specifically with loss. It was designed to equip me and other participants with skills that will enable us to process our own personal grief. I took the class in order to help me cope with the death of my son James. One day the facilitator asked each of us to express in our own words what grief means.

This is what I wrote:

> Death to me is not the end of a person's life. My faith system allows me to consider life after death for those I have lost. I like what an associate of mine said about loss of our loved ones.

> She said in essence that the time we spend with our loved ones when they are living was never meant to continue; however long or short that may be. But when we are united with them at the end of life and the world as we know it, we will spend an eternity with them. Grief for me is different. It clings to me and I now wear it like a well-fitting glove. It ends at the close of my life...

Afterword: Bonus Section

I pray that each chapter of my book has been especially enlightening for you. Maybe you have gotten a glimpse of your own struggles through our stories. Whatever the case may be I trust God to move mountains in your life and that your joy may be full in Him. I hope you remember to "Pay it forward". And oh yes by all means please do enjoy the crumbs I have gathered for everyone in the Bonus Section, which includes Williams' poems, a contribution from James, and some of my poems... Happy reading!

Let the journey begin for all who will partake of the master's crumbs. I pray that as you feast on the offerings from this section you can grab hold of the hope that God gave to my sons James and William in their journey. May you be truly blessed a hundred- fold times over as you gather your own crumbs to continue to carry the torch of hope to others…

Two Places I Have Lived

Two places I have lived are as different as far as the city, weather, and way of living, But one is where I was born and raised the other is home now. When you think about the two places I've lived be it Indianapolis, Indiana or Denver, Colorado, they are different in some aspects. Indianapolis, IN. is in the Midwest whereas Denver, CO., is what is called the Near West. The first used to be home and probably will always be. But the latter is currently home and gets better day by day.

Boykins on the fire again, the headlines read. Earl Boykins finished his previous game with a flurry. Apparently though, he was just getting started. Boykins, on the heels of setting an NBA record for points in overtime, scored 25 points and handed out a season-most 10 assist to lead the Denver Nuggets to a 92-82 win against the Memphis Grizzlies on Friday night at the Pepsi Center. True enough Denver is home of the once Super Bowl champs, the Denver Broncos and the Denver Nuggets led by the young Carmelo Anthony. Sports here in Denver make it easy to be away from my Indianapolis Colts and the all too much famous Indiana Pacers. Like Indianapolis there are truly some diehard fans here in Denver.

The other side of sports is the employment outlook. When I first arrived to Denver in late '03 finding a job was not of my concerns due to the fact I was and still am drawing Social Security Disability. All

I would hear is how the economies were looking bad and no jobs were the complaints. I was lucky to not have to test my job looking skills... Just to be on the right track I enrolled in Parks College (now Everest College) studying Criminal Justice so when I'm ready I would have some cards in my favor.

Living now in what is called the Mile High city has brightened my livelihood. I'm not sure if it's the fresh air or the esteemed mountains that line the west side of the city. Indianapolis was mainly flatlands. I'm sure you've heard there's corn in Indiana. You know you're in Denver when you see duffle bags, bottled water, portable CD players and flip-flops on strangers as they pass you by or sit on the light-rail.

Having health issues that I brought with me from Indy I feel quite healthier here in my present state. When you are born and raised in a location, you tend to get bored with the everyday regimen. Here in Denver I have a small family and no friends. So each day is something new to me whether I leave home or not. I am currently living in the Glendale area. It is almost as far West as I was living East in Indy. As stated earlier attending college at Parks is bound to make my employment easier to find once my educational goals are complete. I like to say I'm on the scenic route to Law school. Once complete I will be a productive citizen of the Mile High.

James H. Williams Jr.

WILLIAM- MAX

They don't make men like they use to. When
I was standing in the assembly line, God said,"
this one is too cool for me ... ". Even the
devil said,"I'll be damn, he even
cracked the mold ••• "
After I'm dead and gone, on my headstone,
"From Sesame Street to Wall Street,
I'm down by Law".
I was taught not to jock, stand out
from the rest Locked up by the bell
Standing on my square.
I'm sucka free, never foolin wit off brands.
I bend for real, never go limp like lettuce.
All head and no br-ass.
I fear no man but God Himself. And That'z
out of respect. What you eat don't Make stuff,
it's what you save ...
When they talk about me I live and let
Die like 007 ... What you believe in
Is fine and dandy. I'll
Tell the "Never-land"
You can't pimp me I'm a· pimp myself ...
Game recognize game. In the ladies eyes,
I'm plain as day.
I'm bright as the "Golden State", layed
back and relaxed. One in a million like
A needle in a haystack.
"Old School", that's the attitude you gots
Ta have to get paid ... It aint what you have
Its what you save.
When they talk a bout me •.. mentality,

Mind straight jacketed on finance.
Educat'n my intelligence.
Handl'n my business.
To live first class. Really Everything Else
Is irrelevant. So Why sweat it Gents?
Cold climate, think fast. Premeditation,
Slow walk.
Knowledge, Street smart., old school, hard knocks.
Stalked by Grand Jurys, never speak. ON
war strokes, pillow talk,
Or horseplay!
I take the game serious about money and
Conduct business. Mo stuff is against
My religion. I keeps it real
And that's that.
Born to put my name on the map. Represent
And leave my mark on the planet. Mo ambitions
Than a pirate captain. Trying to
Build a palace.
Have absolutely no time for play'n ... I'm a
Grown a ... man. Interact with
me, it's gonna be on
An adult level.
Ya gots to be mo careful. I been in some life
threatening situations. Seen 2 much stuff.
I got zero tolerance. A hair trigger,
9 times out of 10.
I'm dressed to kill in hard bottoms. I got All
my cards but I'm get'n old my brotha. My
Nerves is get'n bad.
When you approach me, come at me correct.
Or don't come at me at all. We can have fun ...
Word is "Law"! But it's never personal.

It's always income.
"Cuz" I aint outgoing, I hustle 4 corners fulfill'n
dreams, travel'n the globe. Livin in a material
World of cash Dow.
In the land of plenty-where it's better to have "Mo",
If ya gonna have any. Stay'n off toes, cut'n
No throats, standing strong on the strength,
Slam 'n Cadillac doors
Till I'm old.
Brand new every year as a black man's wish ...
With ultimate the "Master Plan",
I'm in effect. Yall ain't ready 4
"William Max"
But you can't let your right hand see ya left hand.
And stick to the "Master Plan". Be calm and
Collective, and maybe one day, You
Can do the same. Things you wanna do
when you want to- and
Perhaps be as cool as
"William Max"

The Man I Am

The man I am, the path I walk was made for me.
With grains of faith for sand- because of those who paved the way.
I am free to walk this land.
The man [am today warrants not great fame.
The glory lies in the roots I so proudly claim.

WAW aka Knowledge

Night

Four walls. Candles burning in the dark. Visions of bodies in
morgue.

The world is cold as a self-abortion sped up in slow motion.

Woke up one night money on my mind. 9 g's in my hand pants
next to the bed pockets
Flat. Thinking scandalous.

W A W aka Knowledge

Life Is a Trip

Life is a trip filled with choices.
So many decisions to make, I hear voices.
Can't figure out which ones advice I should take.
Stuff comin at me from every angle.
Makes me think, everybody's out for personal gain.

Momma said you aint got no friends.
You can't depend on nobody, look here,
If you make a million dollars it will be a million brothas tryna take what
you got.
Sometimes you gotta back up off the game and peek the object.
For every action, it's an equal and opposite reaction.

To the average, mediocrity is all that.
The beat sounds like a baby rattle.
It's like I'm speaking Japanese, and they only comprehend English.
I'm a green soldier, "host any tribe," speak ebonies and reach all levels of
society.

Cuz, I keep it real.
How good it is.
A word spoken in due sea◇on might save yo life.
Timin is everything.
And your reminder be consequences, like it or not.
Life is a hard pill to swallow on a carbon shot.

The late William A. Williams aka Knowledge

FREDDY'S BACK

Klickity klack, jump back jack.
You've been served, tremble in fear.
Freddy's back!
He's notorious, famous, and glorious.
Most can't see, what will be, will be.
Freddy's back!
He's paying his dues, inside wearing blues.
His game slacking, his time is passing.
Freddy's back!
He did the crime, he did the time.
"Yo", now it's your turn, did you learn?
Freddy's back!
The name is Freddy and, his "Rap" is steady.
They didn't break his will, He's a legend still.
Freddy's back!
Take it from me, this advice is free.
He died a Gee, with a hard core legacy.
Freddy's back!
Take care to avoid his grave at night.
When the moon's full, stay out of sight.
Freddy's back!
When you're in the hood, check behind you.
Don't be a sceptic, it just might be true.
Freddy's back!
Some say it's Freddy that they see,
But Freddy's dead, how can that be?
Did you hear that klickity Klack?
Word, it's Freddy and he's back!
LS Reed

GOT MY BACK TO THE WALL

Back's against the wall.

Life ain't easy; down right sleazy.

Living in a one- room shack.

Nails sticking in my back;

Having a Mack Attack.

Back's against the wall.

Eating that hay; get out my way.

Do some pipe cleaning.

Find some sad meaning,

Weak shoulders leaning.

Back's against the wall.

Got up to frown, work gone down.

Counted plenty a nickel and dime.

My bad, for doing the crime;

Ended up doing the time.

(Lolita Reed Feb. 2003)

LIFE'S FUNNY THAT WAY

When I'm up, you're down
When I'm down, YOU clown.

When I smile, you frown.
When I'm blue, you're brown.

When I bow, you stand.
When I wrap, you band.

When t come, you go.
When t reap, you sow.

When I nickel, you dime.
When I rhyme, you chime.

L.S. Reed

The Rest of My Life

What shall I do with the rest of my life?
A question to ponder when the end is not far,
and there's more of life to see and things to do.

What shall I do with the rest of my life?
The beginning was easier by far.
When the end seemed distant, the future
Bright and unexplored, and life was innocent and new.

What shall I do with the rest of my life?
With each passing year my answer becomes
Quite clear, for I have some regrets, and heaven
Is close in view.

What shall I do with the rest of my life?
I've made a mess of things it's true. But today
Dear Lord, I've cast my lot, and I give
the rest of my life-
To be a sacrifice of praise to You!

(Lolita Reed, 2002)

DON'T KNOW

Robins sing, bluebirds fly, soda- pops,

Grass-hoppers and people die.

I don't know why,

Don't know why,

Don't know why

Boats sail, pop-sickles, skinny-dips,

Mash-potatoes and babies cry.

I don't know why,

Don't know why,

Don't know why

Phones ring, rivers flow, clothes-rack,

Clocks tick, and pie in the sky.

I don't know why,

Don't know why,

Don't know why

Love is blind, cotton-balls, tear-drops,

Push-ups, and he said good-bye.

I don't know why,

Don't know why

Don't know why

(Lolita Reed, January 2003)

I'M A STAR!

"KNOWLEDGE" for a king, long live the Crown. Hail game. Salute the
fearless souls hustlas, pimps and comrades. A moment of silence for the single
mother, and child that slept under a bridge last night.
Respect due to the Addict that quit getting high. Thank God for the shelters and
the Government cheese and food stamps, the soup lines •.. Every night I pray for
a sign. Poor people over seas, the handicapped, the projects.
With the gift of God I make you feel special. Cuz that's what you are •.. I talk to
ya heart to heart.. Cuz ya spark my interest. I'm an exception to the rules, make
ya wanna take off ya shoes .•• Get ya boots knocked and wiggle those pretty little
toes- in the air and talk trash in my ear like ya just don't care •..
I'm not yo average let ya have it yo way and ya take that!!! Say my name
backwards, upside down and when I'm there Ima make it straight smile and
wink at ya. Whoeva holds the belt, all I need is a shot at the title, then I'll be the
champion.
Unordinary, original but not the old run of the mill!
Nah ... I'm a Star!

L.S. Reed

Momma's House on Martindale

Soon as the sun was down the stars came in view.

The lightning bugs swirled about us.

And you can almost smell the warm night's air.

With pure delight we bounded out the door and gathered there.

At momma's house on Martindale.

We could hardly wait for the fun to begin.

Our laughter swelled and our hearts were pounding.

Sometimes we were on top, the team undefeated.

There were times we were the underdogs, at the bottom.

We all played hard, hyped by the sheer fun, and driven by the challenge to win.

Momma was always there, seeing to it that we played fair.

She was a judicious referee.

It didn't matter if we were scratched or bruised.

We all loved to gather there.

At momma's house on Martindale.

Indoors or outside, and week to week.

It was the popular place to be.

Momma decided the curfew, and the games we could play.

Our hearts would sink when it was quitting time.

Just one more time would be our plea.

Then we'd hear momma say, "okay one more time, then like it or not, we'll call it a day."

Perhaps you could recall a game or two.

You may remember some that we both knew.

There were Jacks, Marbles, Jump Rope and Tag.

Remember the hand games back then.

What about "Oh Mary Mack."

Remember Hide and Seek.

There was Red light - Green light.

And oh yes "Lemonade."

Seems like it was only yesterday, we gathered there.

At momma's house on Martindale.

Do you recall those homemade stilts and crushed cans on our shoes?

Rock-school on the steps was popular too.

But indoor games for me were a treat.

The winners sometimes got a prize or candy to eat.

We enjoyed Dominoes, Checkers (both American and Chinese).

It was so much fun to share, when we gathered there.

At momma's house on Martindale.

All sorts of card games we played.

Games like Blackjack, Gin-rummy, Dad-a-Bella and Tonk.

Then there was Solitaire, Bid-Wiz and of course Old Maid.

The funner the game, the longer we stayed.

Board games got our interest too.

There was High Finance and Monopoly.

Fun and games that appealed to me and you.

When we gathered there,

At Momma's house on Martindale.

Those days are fond memories now.

We've aged a little and are all grown up.

Some of us have passed on.

But we all can agree on this one thing.

We will never forget when times were simple

and we had so much fun. Gee those times

were swell. But now it's time to say, "Farewell".

To the times when we all gathered there,

At momma's house on Martindale.

    LS Reed